Active Alcoholism

Table of Contents

Foreword

This is my second book that deals with the ism of alcohol. Again you may have the ism of some other substance such as gambling or drugs or any other problem. The first book dealt with the spirituality of getting sober and staying sober under a power greater than our selves based on spiritual principles of a Christian disposition. I had my own experience which was of a Christian nature, so I used my own experience as the basis of the book. This book will deal with psychological (which basically means the mind) nature of this is illness of mine.

I will try my best to explain how it works in my mind, how I react to it, how I do battle with it and how I can function on a day to day basis in spite of this illness in which I suffer from. I will try my best to explain what is, in essence, a very abstract and obscure disease. I will try my best to humanise it. A sense of humour and a lot of bravery are needed for this. AA in her wisdom has given me the tools to do combat with the illness but again it's up to me to utilise them, I will also lean on psychology as well. "By hook or crook" as they say. This again is based on my own experience, I will use as many real life examples as I can, usually to my own consternation. It's never dull being an alcoholic that doesn't drink and It can be definitely trying at times but the good days outweigh the bad days ten to one. Again, I do this for love of you (the person reading this) the suffering alcoholic, drug addict, gambler and so on. We all need each other, even more so with this illness.

Introduction

"Picture yourself on a boat in a river" yes, I did just use the opening line from lucy in the sky with diamonds, there is a point. If you can imagine yourself in said boat and the river your on is the flow of life (from beginning to end) then this will be our starting point. There will be falls, whirlpools, holes in the boat and some beautiful peaceful moments when it just flows perfectly. This will be us on our journey. Now for the villain of the piece, I think I will use Nessie as the representation of my active alcoholism(I'm Scottish so I really do hope the loch ness monster doesn't hunt me down for using her in such a derogative way.) As your floating down the river every now and then Nessie pops up to your boat and starts with this line of questioning: (For no apparent reason, I've not been fishing for her young or anything like that. She's just really mean.) *are you sure you're an alcoholic? Do you really need AA? Is there really a power greater than yourself?"* and so on and so forth. Thanks Nessie, you've just ruined my day, Bad loch monster. Now imagine you have a hole in your boat or your boats just capsized and your struggling for your very life. This is when Nessie will really try her best to get you "all they people in AA are idiots.... check her out... look at mr wisdom over there... you don't need a sponsor.... just take a wee drink.... Again, thanks Nessie. I love getting kicked when I'm down.

My friends **WELCOME TO ACTIVE ALCOHOLISM.**

Book 1

The Inner Workings Of An
Alcoholic Mind

Prognostication

This is the first dissection into my alcoholic mind. (Please forgive me ahead of time for the use of so many big words, I just found these words and terms best encapsulated what I'm trying to convey to you with the least amount of typing. Where possible I will leave you an explanation. I take easy does it to the extreme even when typing. I'm so lazy.)

Prognostication is the ability to see into the future. Someone with said ability would be a prognosticator, this would be a psychic, a witch doctor or a tea leaf reader or any other of these other fantastical people and now me. Apparently my unconscious mind is under the illusion it has this ability. As on any given day it starts telling me what it's doing next week or tomorrow or some other day. Now it's not someone standing next to me whispering in my ear who is saying this, it's not subliminal messaging (I hope not or I may have to acquire a tin foil hat again to keep the signals out) it's definitely my unconscious mind that the messages are coming from. The conscious part of my mind is when I'm awake in the morning, I'm conscious. Now the next 16 hours that I'm awake, (excluding power napping which we all love, a wee kip in the afternoon is good for the soul.) I'm conscious. That's consciousness (without going into any phenomenological or existential explanation about consciousness, i will probably do that in my next book. So you have been warned).

The unconscious part of my mind from what I can best ascertain runs my body, stores my memories and so on without my active participation in it. The thoughts seems to originate from there. The trigger for it coming into my conscious mind is fear. (The interplay between the conscious and unconscious mind is called psychodynamics, it's like wee mail guys carrying messages back and forth, please don't picture this as you will have nightmares of wee men running about carrying messages back and forth. I spent most of my time getting them drunk which explains why my mind was in such a muddle. Drunken neurons is not a pretty picture).

Now Every human being who has been born or ever will be, once the exuberance of youth has been knock out them and they realise like me the fragility of life, the sheer precariousness of it has a fear of the future, there's not a single human being guaranteed a tomorrow. everyone has a fear of the future. Its vast, uncertain and empty and can change in the blink of an eye. Thats why my mind is trying to fix points in it. If I can know with certainty that I have a tomorrow, then my mind can be at peace. That's probably why a lot of older people harken back to the past, there a solidity and form to your past. Its unchanging and will forever be like that no matter how bad it is. That's also is the eternal part of who your are. Once you are dead and gone your past remains interwoven into human history. As long as there are humans being on planet Earth your past will remain once you have gone. That's a fantastic view of your life but also a warning. AA in her wisdom has given you a chance to write a new past. A new story to be interwoven into the human tapestry.

So fear of the future is natural, but with this disease of mine, it tends to amplify fear out of all proportion thus distorting it. Imagine using a magnifying glass for making small print big. This is the amplification that this disease of mine does to certain emotions. Now all of a sudden fear of the future starts my mind trying to fix points to give it some kind of certainty but what happens is I start thinking "TOMORROW I'LL DO THIS.....NEXT WEEK I'LL BE DOING THIS". By trying to fix points in the future the conscious part of my mind starts thinking about tomorrow "AND TOMORROW I'LL SAY THIS...AND NEXT WEEK I'LL WEAR THIS". So I have to consciously say to myself **"I ONLY HAVE TODAY"** this is my defence against the disease at least pertaining to the prognosticating part of it.

I ONLY HAVE TODAY.

The What If? Massacre

This is my least favourite part of the illness. (I didn't realise I had a favourite part till I started writing this.) Imagine loading a machine gun with "what if? bullets" and firing them all at once. Usually like some kind of fear terrorist invading my conscious mind. It goes a little like this. On any given day, let say I'm at my work and all of a sudden these messages start firing into my conscious mind from my unconscious mind (remember, psychodynamics) in the form of nefarious questions such as   "What if your boss doesn't like you and wishes to get rid of you?" "What if that date your going on Saturday night turns out to be man?" "What if your daughters using drugs?" ad infinitum. Wow, that's a lot to deal with in one thought but that's exactly how this disease works in me, it fires all these questions at me like a fear terrorist.

I have to consciously stop what I'm doing (It now becomes psychosomatic) and I have to decimated part of the AA serenity prayer and then apply it. I have to say to myself "TO ACCEPT THE THINGS I CANNOT CHANGE, THE COURAGE TO CHANGE THE THINGS I CAN AND THE WISDOM TO KNOW THE DIFFERENCE". That's the true wisdom of the serenity prayer. Knowing the things I can and can't change. I cannot change if my boss doesn't like me and wants to get rid of me, that's her choice. I cannot change the fact I may have pulled a crossdressing man rather than a female for my date on Saturday.

(It wouldn't be the first time. When I was a very promiscuous fellow)

I can go to an optician to change that outcome the next time. I definitely cannot change my daughters existential choices in her life. Being the good parent (now I'm sober) I can only ever be there to pick up the pieces when things go terribly wrong and encourage her when they go terribly right. I cannot control the outcome or choices of any of these situations. So **"what if"** can go back to where it came from. Again its fear running riot in my mind or at least the distortion of it through this disease of mine.

Paradoxical Intentions Applied

I was doing this before, I had heard of this terminology. Dr. Viktor E. Frankl is the originator of this terminology through his treatment method of logo therapy. I will use some of his examples then show you how I use paradoxical intentions to help to battle with my illness (for further examples and the further explanations check out Dr. Frankl other books, they are fantastic) he was treating a patient with a case of hysterics and a by product of this was terrible shaking. When he found the patient in the waiting room he decided that he would try and out shake her. At the time she could not hold a cup of tea or even a book. He asked if she would give him a race to see who could shake the fastest and longest. After a short time the poor woman became exhausted and could no longer be bothered to shake. Thus negating her trembling. The sheer absurdity of the situation wasn't lost on her and she began laughing (I too laughed when I read it, laughter is our number one tool to defeat this illness, it brings us out ourselves).

It genuinely helped her, each time he saw her with the shakes he would join her. To face the psychological part of this illness of mine I must too engage this type of thinking. For nearly three years in my sobriety I suffered terrible hallucinations as well as voices. I could see these apparitions as clear as day and could also engage them in conversation. Yippee for me.

My point is, when I first got sober I asked a friend if he would get me holy water and bless my house (I wasn't a Christian back then, I had no theological explanation for this or any psychological one either). These things were never telling me they loved me. In fact it went a bit like this" I'M GOING TO CUT YOUR HEAD OFF AND URINATE IN IT BOY" The joys. I decided it was time to fight back. Most people would have signed them self into a hospital or at least speak to a doctor and get some form of medical relief. I'm not most people (The power greater than our selves decided I needed to learn to relay on him completely, the only time I got a relief from this was in AA meetings and then my church, it was the initial driving force for getting me to church and AA). As soon as I opened my eyes in the morning (became conscious) it started, all the way through till i closed them. That would change the most hardy of souls and it did me, paradoxically I became more loving towards myself and everyone else. So when it became too much I started saying out loud (I'm a headcase, speaking to unseen apparitions is the best way to acquire new friends.

Even in my most heart felt soliloquys I knew I was addressing a power greater than myself) "IS THAT IT? SURELY YOU COULD DO MORE THAN THAT TO ME? WHY NOT TORTURE ME FIRST? YOU COULD HANG ME UPSIDE DOWN OR EVEN BETTER DEATH BY A THOUSAND CUTS". You wouldn't believe how effective this method became. It not only made me laugh but it took away the power from this illness to use fear to intimidate me.

When I went down on my knees at night to say thank you for another day sober it usually would tell me all the terrible things I'd done and I would reply " I'VE DONE MUCH WORSE THAN THAT, YOUR IS ROTTEN AND OUT OF DATE, YOUR SLACKING BOYO". This is how I was able to produce a more than capable coping system to deal with this illness at its very worst. I heard a man say one night in a meeting that when he gets a racing mind he goes and grabs a high sugar energy drink to speed it up. This is the application of paradoxical intentions to deal with our day to day living. When your head is in a bad state ask for more if you dare, believe me it works. By imagining the problem to get even worse I try to blow it out of all proportion and it becomes ridiculous also quite funny. Its makes me laugh when I try to do it. One instance, I was phoning in sick (Everybody hates doing that) so I got a bit panicky about it, so I said to myself "what if they don't believe me and decide to sack me".

Then I went further, What if instead of sacking me they decide to flog me to make an example of me, what if they go even further and decide to crucify me like my lord (did you notice that the fear terrorist had jumped into my mind again with the "what if?" machine gun again) This got me laughing and took away the power of fear before it took off. Fear followed by anxiety and all other kinds of neurotic behaviour start to occur if I let it. So I fight fire with fire and this helps me immensely. I really would give it a shot my friend. Be brave and fearless about it. Take charge of it. Instead of trying to fight these feelings, embrace them and then try to outdo them. It really does work.

For a more in depth explanation I really would recommend the good Dr. Frankyl's books for it. I have tried to simplify it for you and give you some practical applications in your day to day living but it's up to you to be brave. You can be and I trust you will be.

Fantasy Island, Occupant 1 (Me)

Now to the next part of this very excitable mind of mine. Imagination. It goes a little like this. I'm up my local super market and I see a girl walking towards me. I look at her, she looks at me, our eyes interlock and I draw her a smile, and then she smiles back. Bang, instantaneously I buy a train ticket to fantasy island. My first thought is "she fancies me", next thought "she will look me up on Facebook and then proceed to send me a friends request" next thought "then we will go out on a date" then "she will probably want to move in" and so on. All that one smile, I must be the best poker player in history. But this is exactly my train of thinking (hence the reason for a train ticket, I was trying to be funny... tumble weed rolling by). There are two things which pertain to me on this train ticket. Number 1 is my ego, I struggle sometimes with a crippling self confidence. This illness of mine has a great habit of reaching into my memories and showing me something which I was I had forgot.

My past may be my greatest asset but my illness loves to go their and find some deep, dark forgotten memory. So when that happens I usually feel lower than a snake so I have to puff my ego out of all proportion (the amplification thing again) so know I'm lying in the gutter looking down on people again, of course she looking at me cause she fancies me, apparently everybody does, the whole worlds all about me again, me, me,me...

The second thing on the ticket to fantasy island that pertains to me is loneliness. I have lived myself for a great number of years and every human being feels loneliness but it's the amplification of it that blows it out of all proportion and totally distorts it. So I'm not just lonely, I'm the only guy left in the universe. "where did you all go?". The currency that I used to buy this train ticket to fantasy island is fear. The number one tool this illness of mines uses against me. I may sound as if I'm giving fear a bad wrap but believe me fear can be healthy. Its when this illness of mine gets a hold of fear and blows it out of all proportion. It becomes distorted and unruly and totally fantastical. Fear itself is healthy, when someone throws a brick at you fear will make you duck. That's a very wise thing to do, it's healthy and self preserving, that's the fear of the lord I have in my own faith. It keeps me out of trouble for the best part, not always. I'm a very broken human being some days and just being a human functioning normally is hard enough. So fear amplified through my disease buys me a ticket to fantasy island. Believe me when I tell you that I have bought that ticket so many times they send me offers for being a frequent visitor.

Scientific Theory Verus Hypothesis

What the hell does this have to do with the ism? You may be thinking by now you are dealing with a mad man. You'd be right. I'm an honest mad man but mad all the same. Here's a view of how my mind works that you may wish to implement into your own day to day living or at least try as I do. If your not familiar with scientific theory it works a little like this. Imagine if you will a tree. The roots of the tree will be strands of evidence. The trunk of the tree will be the good data collected to support it (usually lots of testing and stuff) and the roof of the tree (the part with the leaves and the little birds nest) will be the conclusion. Scientific theory is not just a theory and no, it's not a truth either, it's kind of in the middle.

There can be parts that change in it though time which may change the conclusion but until then It remains our best explanation for how something works until we find a new and better one. It's a fantastic way of training your mind how to think. Small evidence, good data and then a conclusion. I wish my mind worked like that. This is how my mind really works most times. By hypothesising. It works a little like this. A scientist approaches me (this happens all the time. I'm sure your familiar with a scientist chapping your door to sell you his latest theory. If not then it's just like those pesky sales people.) and tells me that he's found evidence of life on mars. I tell him that not only that there was life on mars but sometime in the not too distant past, a bi pedal, humanoid civilisation lived there. His response" *really? Where did you get that from? No I cant believe that, just from that piece of evidence. Where's your good data supporting it?*". I went from the roots of the tree to the top without getting a trunk to support my theory. It will remain in the hypothesis stage. It's not to say it isn't true, there's just not enough supporting evidence to make it a theory. This is exactly how my mind works. Always jumping to conclusion without any good evidence to support, I go straight from the roots to the top of the tree. If I can applicate scientific theory to my thinking I would be much more successful in my day to day living.

When I have a problem or a thought with no evidence it's up to me to gather the evidence in to support my theories (in which I have loads). If it's a family issue I can phone the person involved, speak to other members or even my sponsor for some outside advise. This would be me gathering evidence. Instead of just jumping to conclusions (all the time). This again takes time to formalise in your own mind. It needs to be practised all the time until it becomes part of your new nature. It'll become your second nature.

Book 2

AA And Her Wisdom

My Past Is My Greatest Asset Really?

Really? Are you sure? Honestly? My past? Its hell on wheels! At which point can that ever be an asset?. When I heard someone say that their past is their greatest asset I nearly choked myself with laughter. My own past was like a millstone round my neck. It chocked the life out of me. I dragged it everywhere I went. It was raw, painful and full of hate and sorrow, regret and every other bit of darkness a man can collect in his life unchecked. So how could I possibly utilise that mess? Unbelievably I did. I tell you a little bit about how my past was at first my greatest weakness and then became my greatest strength. You are only as sick as your secrets. You have probably heard this before but I'll explain why. By repressing our unwanted memories and all other things I would rather forget it becomes a somewhat metaphorical boil in my mind, and because I'm trying to suppress past traumatic events rather than deal with them they become psychosomatic. They start revealing themselves in different kinds of neurosis such as anxiety, depression, agitation and so on. Without dealing with past traumatic events they fester away inside my mind, by adding drink and drugs to the situation, I begin to exacerbate an already damaged mind, It wasn't long before neurotic behaviour became psychotic. A very fine line. I was sexually abused as a boy but I never told anyone, I tried to block it out. What occurred was a life of hell. I missed most of my education, I took drugs, I drank, I tried to kill myself so many times that it became farcical.

By trying to repress my secrets I became both physically and mentally sick. The extended abuse of alcohol and drugs turned my neurotic behavior into psychotic. It was horrific for me and anybody who had the unfortunate chance of loving me.

I became as sick as my secrets. This was the chief weight in my own millstone and it was heavy. I dragged it around with me all the time, never realising the affect it was having on my own being. So how could I possibly use a life time of hurt, pain and misery and alcohol misuse to my advantage? It's so easy it's scary. Since I got sober (I say me but I truly believe in my heart that the lord Jesus did it for me) I've had some pretty crappy days where I just really struggled but in all truth they have never been as bad as any of my past days. The desperation of not having drink, having to steal and so on . Struggling to even feed myself and so on. My worst days in sobriety are nowhere near anything like my normal days in my past. I have a reference point now.

When I'm struggling I can flip my memory back to some awful day I had and draw a comparison with my current struggles and find out that it really not as bad as that. So instead of being a milestone round my neck it becomes a hammer, to smash my current cycle of fear induce problems. If I'm just about to lose my job which I did one xmas time, I did what I always do now. I say to myself "well, it's not as bad as waking up with no power or food in my house, I will get through this" I did that Christmas.

I volunteered at the food bank and I got a true perspective of people a lot worse off than me. Use your past as a driving force to push you on to much greater things.

I never imagined when I was standing outside the local shops begging for £1 for a bottle of cider I would be here writing this book for you. I'm a miracle and so are you. I promise you if you stay clean you will have the greatest time of your life. That past of mine is nothing in comparison to my future. It's my driving force for good, it's my reference point for when things go bad (I was just thinking maybe I could have had an even more terrible past and it would be an even greater propelling force, another practical application for using paradoxical intentions).it will never be as bad as that. It truly is mine and your greatest asset.

Picking Up the Pieces For The Right Jigsaw

Assimilation and implementation of the 12 step program into your life is one of the most beautiful things to ever happen to me. It worked a lot like a master reset of my inner core. Very similar to the app on my phone that resets my phone back to factory settings.

First and foremost I had to restart my whole life on a new set of principles as well as new way of thinking. The growing pains in AA are horrific, just paying a bill was new to me, trying to live on a budget, food shopping and so on. I had to learn it all over again. How to deal with life on life terms is still an ongoing battle but if you give it time it will become your second nature. Now in regards to the pieces, I will start at the beginning. Through the traumatic events which was to shape my childhood I became lost (I was sexually abuse as a ten year old boy) so now I felt different from my friends and sure as hell didn't want to think differently, so I began just trying to assimilate myself into this world and conform to its image of what it meant to be a man. This meant picking up the wrong pieces of the jigsaw and piecing together the wrong picture. Instead of applying myself to school I skipped it with my friends, instead of saying no to drink and drugs I said yes, instead of not fighting with people I did that too. All these things I never wished to do as they went against my inner me but I was a horrific people pleaser.

I felt different so I didn't want to stand out from the crowd. Drink and drugs would help piece together this unholy picture which I was to become. I hated me for being so weak and I hated me for not being able to express who I truly was. I just couldn't snap out the cycle in which I was in from my childhood. i was still trying in my late thirties until I got sober.

I got stuck with this image of myself which was all wrong. I was trying to be someone I wasn't and the result was my inner life was destroyed and my outer life became my main place of action. I use to wear different faces for different places. I put on one face for my family, one for my mates. One for the world and somewhere in between that, I got lost. By mismatching my outer against my inner life, it killed it. I would kid on I was round to see my mum but really wishing to get money from her. I would kid my mates on when out I was a big hardman but the whole time I was a coward. I would spend time with my daughters acting like the doting dad the whole time wanting to ditch her to go for a drink. Everything I said or did back then was visceral. Think, think, think was a trillion miles away back then, it still can be now. I learned who I really was when I came into AA but more in important who I was not. I'm not a hardman, a thief, a conman, a cheat, a gangster or any other sort of thing that the world glorified. I'm first and foremost, very broken. That was my starting point.

I was more likely to love someone than hate them. I found out I like helping other people rather than harming. I was learning for the first time how my inner life was more important than my outer. To be true to yourself. I learned to speak from my heart. I learned to care for others. I began to educate myself about who and what, I really am. What makes me tick and so on. I picked the first and most important pieces of this new jigsaw from AA and I began to piece together who I really was. Some of it I loved, some of it I hated but it made the overall a picture complete. The good and the bad . I learned to be at peace with who I am and more importantly who I am not. I learned to change the bits I didn't like. It takes time to find the bad bits then change them, little by little. The new image

I had was the true image of what I was. I became the person I always dreamed I could be but never had the courage or strength to be. These are the two truths in my life that are unchangeable. Number one is i'm an alcoholic, there's no changing that. That's my first step as soon as I wake up is to admit to myself I'm alcoholic. Number two is my faith. Its unchanging too. One is my greatest weakness the other is my greatest strength. I vacillate between both in a day to day basis. The two certainties in my life that will never change until i draw my last breathe then I live for eternity in my greatest strength. My lord and my saviour, Jesus Christ though after reading this he may want to shove me on a cloud all on my own for eternity just to get peace. I love you dearly my friend and so does he. Until we get home my friend, may god guide and love you always.

Conclusion

This has been a journey of a heuristic nature of me, in which I am the benefactor. It had to be that way. I really had be left the tools to find my own way of utilising them. The tools AA has given me and also my own faith have been sitting there waiting for me to utilise them. The people in the fellowships and my church could help me to a point but for the other 20 hours a day I had to learn how to deal with life on life's terms. I have leaned heavily on AA and her wisdom and on that power greater than ourselves whom I choose to call the Jesus. I really hope the insight I have given you into my own mind can help you in some way to make you feel that you are no longer alone. I may never meet you but believe me when I tell you that I love you. That's why I do these books, it's always for love. That's what I was given, so in turn I can give it away to you. It's not easy having this disease as it centres in the mind but this is the burden life has lain on my shoulders. There are people out there with much heavier burdens than I will ever carry and they do that unbelievably well. To them I dedicate my time, effort, prayers and my love. To you also I offer my time, effort, prayers and most important my love for you. You may not feel it right now but you will. Know this, if you have had the misfortune of reading this book then it's because I prayed that it would find you and let you know that you are no longer alone(god has a sense of humour too). Love is the highest ideal that any human can aim for.

It's more important than university degrees, than the biggest house, the most money and so on. Love is what it is all about. If I don't have it, then everything I ever have or achieve is useless. May the power greater than ourselves love and guide you always and forever.

Bibliography

Frankl, Viktor E. *Man's Search for Meaning*.
Boston: Beacon, 2006. Print.

Frankl, Viktor E. *The Unheard Cry for Meaning:
Psychotherapy and Humanism*. New York: Simon
and Schuster, 1978. Print.

Richards, Dean. *Psychology in Plain English*.
Place of Publication Not Identified: Createspace
Independent, 2012. Print.

Holy Bible: New International Version. N.p.: n.p.,
n.d. Print.

www.ingramcontent.com/pod-product-compliance
Lightning Source LLC
Chambersburg PA
CBHW061946280526
45787CB00004B/1740